How to Hire your Wedding Vendor

Dream Team

A Book of Interview Questions on: What to ask your service providers before you hire them.

Providing an easy and organized way to compare the potential service providers you may hire for your Big Day.

From Green-Eyed Girl Productions
Cover Image Credit: Kelsea Joann Photography | www.kelseajoann.com

Congratulations!

You're engaged!

As soon as those first few blissful months of engagement are over, there is some serious planning to be done. Though the little details and accents may be the most fun to plan, some very big decisions must be made as soon as possible. Early planning and decision making, such as choosing those who will help you, will make your entire experience more enjoyable. You will need to contact, make appointments and have meetings with venues, photographers, and even travel agents so that you are taken care of by the very best on your wedding day.

…But what in the world do you ask them when you do meet? There are just so many questions and you don't want to forget something important!

For that…you have this book…

Notes on the Author and Green-Eyed Girl…

My name is Kandice Kelso and I have been planning and coordinating large events and weddings, for many years. You know the kid who gets involved with every function in high school; homecoming, fundraiser carnivals, pageants. That kid was me! I am a certified Wedding Professional through the American Association of Wedding Professionals (AA-WP), which has tremendously helped build further knowledge and understanding of the wedding industry.

Over the years I have noticed a pattern developing among my brides and couples. At our post wedding follow up meetings they would all share the same feeling… that the one most overwhelming part of their planning was the process of finding, deciding on and hiring their vendors. Using my education from AA-WP and many other instructional guides, I decided to compose this workbook as a reference for couples everywhere for this specific purpose. This book is not a "wedding organizer" but a facilitator of questions and answers in one consolidated location.

You can read more about me and Green-Eyed Girl Productions on our Coordinating Blog. www.green-eyedgirlproductions.com

Table of Contents...

How to use this Book...

This book is meant to assist you in the interview process with the service providers (vendors) you may hire for your wedding day. The wedding planning process, meant to be fun and exciting, can quickly become overwhelming if you do not employ the vendors best suited for your needs, personality and style. This book is designed with each specific vendor receiving their own section of interview questions. Vendors include everyone involved with your wedding from the ceremony site to the cake bakery.

Each section allows for the business information of two different vendors who will be interviewed on separate occasions. The columns are set side by side to make for an easy comparison after the interviews. Pre-read each section before heading into your interview and <u>Write answers on the pages!</u> That *is* why you have them.

The lists of questions are not meant to be copied off and handed to a vendor, but kept together and in your own handwriting so that they are easily accessible.
Though questions ranges may vary for some vendors, interviews do not have to include every question. Before your interviews, you and your fiancé should go over each list of questions and select the ones that most apply to your wedding.
Highlight them! You will want to ask both vendors the same questions so that your comparisons are accurate. For the sake of efficiency, an interview should not be shorter than 10 questions or longer than 90 minutes. However, depending on the depth of answers you receive, you may need to ask some follow up questions to be satisfied with the responses. Never leave an interview without answers to all of the questions YOU want answered! In fact, the first 10 questions in each column are the ones that I suggest you ask everyone. I have also left room at the end for you to add in your own questions.

Where to start...

Begin by asking your friends and family about the vendors who helped them with their weddings and get some word-of-mouth referrals. Also, do your own research online through local wedding directories and visit some wedding professionals' websites. Preview as many vendors as you like! Around 9-12 months prior to your Big Day, gradually narrow your choices down to the top two vendors you want to interview. Select a third as a backup in case one of your top two is already booked for your date. **Call your vendors and see if they are available on your wedding date before ever scheduling an interview.** If

Above and Beyond...

Consider marking the questions with different colored highlighter pens. Color code based on a priority scale from high to low. At the interview ask questions according to your priority scale. That way if time runs outs, you have already asked the important stuff!

Above and Beyond...

Selecting your vendors:
Attend a Bridal Show in your area and collect a whole bunch of business cards. Organize by categories and use the business cards to help you make a "top picks" list. You and your fiancé can lay everything out on the dining room table and decide together on the top two.

they are available, ask them if you and your fiancé can set up a meeting with them about your wedding. Let them know you will be bringing in a list of questions for them to answer. Set up a time where both you and your fiancé can attend each separate interview, with at least 90 minutes for a face-to-face sit down. Be sure to bring along any photos or magazine clippings you have collected to show them your style, ideas and inspirations. And of course...Bring your Interview Book!

Before an interview...

Read through each list of questions before you head into the interview, perhaps a few days before. If any question does not pertain to your wedding cross it off the list completely. Next, highlight the questions you really want answered. You may like a lot of the questions and want to ask them all, which is okay, but that should be determined by the pace of the interview. Again, for the sake of time and efficiency try to keep all of your interviews under 90 minutes. If your vendor is providing fast, precise answers, ask away.

Conducting an Interview...

Respect. Many of us Wedding Professionals are small business owners and love what we do. You are important to us. Avoid going into interviews asking for discounts.
{We know you know that ☺ #endrant}

When you meet with vendors, introduce yourselves and allow them to give you their "pitch" before you dive into your well-prepared list of questions. Listen carefully as the pitch may answer some of your questions, and you won't need to ask them again. When the pitch has finished, remind them that you brought some questions of your own that need to be answered. At that time, you may pull out your list and begin asking your highlighted questions. When you come to one that was already answered either fill it in quickly, or skip it and fill it in after the interview. Remember to watch the clock and keep your interview on track with respect for your time and theirs.

There is no one right way to ask these questions. You may go in any order you want, skip around and, of course, omit asking any certain question. If you are not comfortable asking about deposits and money first, save it for the end. Or if the vendors' pitch leads you in to a different section, go with the flow. Remember that a simple yes or no will do for many questions, but if you want them to elaborate, politely ask them to do so and then move on to the next question when you receive a satisfactory explanation.

Smile and have fun! Remember that they've probably done hundreds of interviews just like this. So, if you're nervous, just let them lead the way. They want to help you on your biggest day ever and they're pretty awesome at it... which is probably why you're interviewing them!

You will do great! Best of Luck,
The Green-Eyed Girl

The Wedding Site

Things to consider before scheduling an interview with your ceremony site and reception site:

- Location, location, location:
    - Is it big enough to accommodate our guest list?
    - Is the venue easy to find and reasonably close to hotels or mass transit systems?
    - Is there a wedding night suite?
    - Is the space suitable for our time of year and the weather?
- Will the gardens and scenery be pleasant looking in the spring or fall months?
    - Does it fit your vision? A bold black and fuchsia may not jive with a little barnyard...

Questions to ask about a Ceremony Site...

Option 1: _____   Option 2: _____
Contact Name: _____   Contact Name: _____
Contact Number: _____   Contact Number: _____
Appointment date/time: _____   Appointment date/time: _____

Questions	Option 1	Option 2
What is the site fee?		
How many hours/days does that fee cover?		
Is use of the site for rehearsal covered in the site fee?		
Is there a deposit required to reserve this site? What is the percentage?		
Are there any cleaning or maintenance deposits?		
Are those deposits refundable if we clean up the following morning?		
When will we need to pay the balance?		
Could you outline your cancellation policy?		
How many people does the space hold? Seated and Standing? Is it wheelchair accessible?		
Will someone be there to help coordinate the rehearsal?		

Will someone on site manage the deliveries and vendor direction on the Big Day?		
Is there someone on staff to help with the day of events?		
Is there parking? What is the capacity?		
Will you host more than one wedding on the same day? Same time?		
Where do the wedding parties get dressed?		
Where would we set up a welcome & gift table?		
Do you provide chairs & table(s)?		
How long is the aisle?		
Will vows be heard without a microphone? Is one available just in case?		
Will the Officiant need a microphone?		
Does the venue have liability insurance?		
Do we need to purchase any additional insurance policies?		
Is there a plan for inclement weather? An indoor alternative?		

When can we get into the site to decorate?		
When must we take down any decorations?		
Can we hang decorations from the ceiling?		
Are there any "open flame" restrictions on candles?		
Are ceremony tossers allowed? (birdseed, etc)		
Where are formal pictures taken before the ceremony?		
Can we bring in musicians to play their instruments?		
Where would musicians set up for the ceremony?		
Are there enough electrical outlets to support their power needs?		
Have you ever blown a fuse? Was it fixed timely?		
What is the biggest problem you have had with this site? How was it resolved?		
Can you hear any distracting noises during our ceremony time? Highway, animals?		
Are there any recently married couples who used this site that we can call to discuss the venue?		

Can you refer us to any vendors you have worked with? Are there any vendors we have to work with if we use this site?		

If a House of Worship		
Must we both be members of this church to have our wedding here?		
Will you allow weddings on any day of the week or are we restricted to any particular days?		
Is there a fee for renting the church or is a donation acceptable?		
Will guests of another religion be allowed to attend our ceremony if it is held in this church?		
Do you allow photography and video during the ceremony?		
Can we bring in our own flowers? Will they need to be donated to the church? Or can we take them?		
Are other decorations permitted?		
Do you ever allow non-religious services?		

Questions to ask about a Reception Site...

Option 1: _____   Option 2: _____
Contact Name: _____   Contact Name: _____
Contact Number: _____   Contact Number: _____
Appointment date/time: _____   Appointment date/time: _____

	Option 1	Option 2
What is the site fee?		
How many hours/days does that fee cover?		
Is use of the site for rehearsal the night before covered in the site fee?		
How many of those hours are meant for setup/cleanup?		
Will overtime charges apply if we stay longer?		
Is there a deposit required to reserve this site? What is the percentage?		
Are there any cleaning or maintenance deposits?		
Are those deposits refundable if we clean up the following morning?		
When will we need to pay the balance? Do you accept credit cards?		

Could you outline your cancellation policy?		
Can you give us an overview of your unique services?		
How many people does the space hold? Seated and Standing?		
Is there an on-site coordinator?		
Will someone on site manage the deliveries and vendor direction on the Big Day?		
Is there someone on staff to help cue the day of events?		
Will you ever do more than one reception on the same day? Same time?		
Is there another event scheduled on our date?		
Is there an event prior to our time that is using the space we're looking at?		
How are these events managed to make sure the day runs smoothly?		
Does the venue have liability insurance? What does it cover?		

Do we need to purchase any additional insurance policies?		
Is there a plan for inclement weather? An indoor alternative?		
Is there parking? What is the capacity?		
Is valet available? What is extra charge?		
Can we hire an outside valet service?		
Where would we set up a welcome & gift table?		
Do you provide a tables & chairs? What all does the site provide?		
How many guests fit per table (if provided)?		
Are tables and chairs easily setup? Who does this?		
Is the ground level enough to set out tables & chairs?		
How does flow work if several areas are used?		

If used for ceremony & reception, where will they each take place?		
How will the room be transformed? How long will that take?		
Is there a caterer?		
If not, is there a kitchen for a caterer to use?		
Is there a particular caterer we have to use?		
Are there any time restrictions on music?		
Are there rules about volume and hours that music is played?		
Is there room for a band/DJ to set up? Where would it be?		
Can we bring in musicians to play their instruments?		
If we hire a band or musicians, where would they set up?		
Are there ample electrical outlets to support their needs?		

Have you ever blown a fuse? Was it fixed?		
Is there enough room for a dance floor? Where will it be?		
What is your dance floor's capacity?		
Are the areas wheelchair-accessible?		
Where are the bathrooms located? How many stalls?		
Is there an attendant? What is the extra fee?		
If no bathrooms, is there room for portable toilets? Do we need to rent portable toilets?		
Are other spaces (gardens, terraces) accessible to guests?		
Are there extra fees for these spaces?		
Are there any spaces that are off limits?		
Where are cocktails usually served?		

Is it a public space where anybody can wonder in & out?		
Is the space air-conditioned or heated?		
Are there decorations we can use? Are other decorations permitted?		
When could we get into the site to decorate?		
When must we take down any decorations?		
Is there security on-site or in the parking lot?		
Are there any "open flame" restrictions on candles?		
Are there any recently married couples who used this site that we can call to discuss the venue?		
Can you refer us to any vendors you like to work with?		
Are there any vendors we have to work with if we use this site?		
What is the biggest problem you have had? How was it resolved?		

Questions to ask an Officiant...

Option 1: _____   Option 2: _____
Contact Name: _____   Contact Name: _____
Contact Number: _____   Contact Number: _____
Appointment date/time: _____   Appointment date/time: _____

	Option 1	Option 2
Please give us an outline of your services?		
Is there a fee, or is a donation acceptable?		
Are you our religion?		
How many wedding services have you preformed?		
Would you attend the wedding rehearsal?		
How long is the typical ceremony you perform?		
Can we write our own vows? If so would you give us guidelines?		
Could we personalize the ceremony?		
Can we include family members to perform songs, readings?		

If interfaith marriage, Can we have another Officiant take part in the service?		
Would you perform the ceremony outside a house of worship?		
If the wedding is out of town will you travel?		
Will you give a sermon? Can we see a copy before the wedding?		
What is expected of us for premarital courses?		
How many pre-marital meetings could we plan to have with you?		
Do you ever perform non-religious services?		
Is there a deposit required to reserve your services for our date?		
When and where would we sign the marriage certificate?		
Are there any requirements regarding who can be a witness?		
Will you ever do more than one service a day?		

Getting Organized

Things to consider before scheduling an interview with a Wedding Coordinator and Rental Company:

Weigh these options before an interview so that you have an idea of the packages you need.

- Does he/she make you comfortable or ease your mind? You will be spending a lot of time with this person!
- Evaluate exactly where you need help with the planning and how it will fit into your budget before the meeting.
- Is a representative easy to talk to and visit with on a one-on-one level?
- Can you setup your exact table display before committing to any rentals? Can you see pictures of all items?

Questions to ask a Wedding Coordinator...

Option 1: _____   Option 2: _____
Contact Name: _____   Contact Name: _____
Contact Number: _____   Contact Number: _____
Appointment date/time: _____   Appointment date/time: _____

	Option 1	Option 2
What is your style?		
Can we see a portfolio of your work?		
Are you a Certified Wedding Coordinator? Through which association?		
Do you have a business license? How long have you been in business?		
Could you give us an overview of your services?		
What is your fee? Do you charge hourly, by a package rate or a percentage of the total wedding budget?		
What services are available and at what charges for our date?		
Can we create our own package of your services to best fit our needs?		
Can we hire you to plan the entire event?		

Can we hire you to help with just some of the planning?		
Can we hire you to facilitate on the Big Day only?		
How many hours would you be at our event?		
What details do you handle?		
What details will you not handle?		
How many other events would you be organizing that day?		
How many people from your staff would be at the wedding?		
Can we hire additional staff to work that day?		
How long has your staff worked for you?		
Who cleans up our wedding on the next morning? Can we hire you to do that?		
How many meetings should we plan to have with you?		

Are you available to conference over the phone or email?		
Have you planned any weddings at our venue before?		
Do you know the catering director or site manager for our venue?		
Do you have vendors you have worked with in the past that you highly recommend?		
Are there vendors that you require us to use?		
Do these vendors offer your clients discounts?		
What would the process be for hiring vendors for our wedding?		
Is there a deposit required to reserve your services for our date? What is the percentage?		
When will we need to pay the balance? Do you accept credit cards?		
Could you outline your cancellation policy?		
Do you have liability insurance? What does it cover?		

If you are ill, who will coordinate our wedding?		
Do you coordinate weddings primarily?		
What other events do you coordinate?		
What will you wear?		
Do you and your staff require meals?		
Are there any additional charges? (Travel, etc.)		
How do you cope with last minute changes?		
How many weddings do you coordinate a year?		
Can you refer us to any vendors you've worked with in the past?		
What is the biggest problem you have had? How was it resolved?		
Can you provide a list of references that have recently used your services?		

Questions to ask an Event Rental Company & Stylist...

Option 1: _____   Option 2: _____
Contact Name: _____   Contact Name: _____
Contact Number: _____   Contact Number: _____
Appointment date/time: _____   Appointment date/time: _____

	Option 1	Option 2
Can we see a portfolio of your rental inventory?		
Can your inventory accommodate the size of our guest list?		
Do you have a business license? How long have you been in business?		
Could you give us an overview of your services?		
What services are available and at what charges for our date?		
Can we come pick up and return everything ourselves? What dates and times?		
Will you ship to an out-of-town or state site?		
Do you deliver? At what rate per mile?		
When are items delivered? How soon before our event and when are they due back?		

Are there extra charges for off delivery dates? For example on holidays.		
How many hours are the rentals in our possession with the set fee?		
Are extensions available if we want to have them sooner or longer?		
Are there late fees if items are not returned within the allotted time?		
Do you offer a variety of selections in different price ranges?		
Do you offer a variety of tent styles and sizes?		
Do you offer table linens in different fabrics, textures and colors?		
Do you offer china, flatware, glassware, and serving ware in different patterns or colors?		
Do you offer any other items we may need?		
Is there anyone on staff to help us achieve the look we want?		
What are the fees for the specific items we want? (Reference List A)		

How does setup work? Is there an additional fee for that?		
How does breakdown work? Is there an additional fee?		
How does the payment schedule work? Is there a breakage or damages deposit?		
Will we get our deposit back if there are no damages? Who determines the level of damages and what was there already before?		
When will we need to pay the balance? Do you accept credit cards?		
Could you outline your cancellation policy?		
Do you have liability insurance? What does it cover?		
Until what deadline can we make changes to or cancel our order without penalty?		
Is there an emergency contact number in case items are not delivered or arrive damaged?		
Can you refer us to any vendors you've worked with in the past?		
Can you provide a list of references that have recently used your services?		

The Candids

Things to consider before scheduling an interview with your photographers and videographers:
Weigh these options before an interview so that you have an idea of the packages you need

1. What is important to you for Photography?
    - Pictures of you getting ready, the ceremony, the reception, the after party?
    - What do you want to get out of it?
        1. Tons of prints? Elegant albums? Unique favors? CD slideshow? Parent albums?
2. What is important to you for Videography?
    - Footage of you getting ready, just the ceremony or reception, everything, a day of edit played at the cocktail hour or reception
    - Videos for your family, parents, attendants?

Questions to ask a Photographer...

Option 1: _____   Option 2: _____
Contact Name: _____   Contact Name: _____
Contact Number: _____   Contact Number: _____
Appointment date/time: _____   Appointment date/time: _____

	Option 1	Option 2
Could you give us an overview of your services?		
Can we create our own package of your services to best fit our needs?		
How long have you been in business?		
What services are available and at what charges?		
How many hours would you be at our event?		
Is there a deposit required to reserve your services for our date? What is the percentage?		
When will we need to pay the balance? Do you accept credit cards?		
Could you outline your cancellation policy?		
Do you have liability insurance? What does it cover?		

If you are ill, who will photograph our wedding?		
Do you photograph weddings primarily?		
What is your style?		
Can we see an album of one entire wedding?		
Can we see a portfolio of your work? Can we see indoor and outdoor shots?		
Do you bring back up equipment?		
Will you provide an Engagement Shoot? Is there an extra fee?		
How soon would we get to see the proofs of our Engagement shoot?		
Would you provide a Portrait with mat for guests to sign?		
Can we get our Save-the Dates from you?		
What other wedding styles you have done in?		

What other types of photography have you done or still do?		
How many meetings will we have with you?		
Do you use a digital camera or film? What quality and brand of film do you use?		
Approximately how many shots are taken?		
How many proofs do we get to see?		
When do you first start photographing?		
How is "face time" divided into the photos per person?		
Will you work off a prepared shot list?		
Can we give you a list of people we want shots of?		
Can we give you a list of people we DON'T want pictures of?		
Will you work with a Family Liaison if we provide one?		

How do overtime charges work, if any?		
Do you have a formal education in photography? Where did you acquire your education?		
Will you shoot at the rehearsal and dinner? What is that fee?		
Will you come early on the day of to photograph us getting ready? Is that included in the fee or is that extra?		
Will you shoot black & white as well as color?		
Were the photos we're looking at developed at the same place, by the same person who would develop ours?		
Do you retouch images? Is there an extra fee?		
Do you capture key events from separate angles; with 2+ cameras? If not, is that an option?		
Do you use a tripod or stationary camera for the ceremony?		
How many cameras will you bring?		
Do you ever zoom in?		

Will you create a slideshow to play at the reception if we provide you pictures? Is there an extra fee?		
Do you have equipment for that? Screen/projector?		
How soon would you need the footage to put that together for us?		
Could we use your equipment if we make our own montage?		
How many photographers and assistants would be at our wedding?		
If others are shooting can we see their work?		
What will you wear?		
Do you and your staff require meals? How many others will you bring on the Big Day?		
Are there any additional charges? (Travel, etc.)		
How do you cope with last minute changes?		
How many weddings do you photograph a year?		

Do you have different lens you use to shoot different lightings?		
Can you refer us to any vendors you've worked with in the past?		
What is the biggest problem you have had? How was it resolved?		
Can you provide a list of couples that have used your services?		

Prints, Packages & Albums		
	Option 1	Option 2
How many images are included in the cost?		
How long after we make our selections will we get the prints or albums?		
What is the cost for each additional album?		
How many pictures are in each album? Can we add pages? What is the cost to add?		
What are the size options for portraits?		
How many portraits are included in the fee? What is the cost for additional prints?		
How soon will we get to see proofs?		

Do we have choices for album, and page styles?		
Is there an extra fee to print our names and date on the album cover?		
Are there any other novelty items you offer?		
Do we get to keep the proofs and/or negatives as part of the package?		
If not, can we purchase them, or will you always own them?		
If you keep the negatives, for how long do you keep them?		
Can we get a digital slideshow (DVDr) of our proofs and/or prints?		
Will we have unlimited print rights?		
Will you edit (retouch) all the proofs, or just the ones we order?		
Do you offer smaller parent/party albums? Is there an extra fee?		
Can you set up a photo booth for guests during cocktail hour/reception?		

Questions to ask a Videographer...

Option 1: _____ Option 2: _____
Contact Name: _____ Contact Name: _____
Contact Number: _____ Contact Number: _____
Appointment date/time: _____ Appointment date/time: _____

	Option 1	Option 2
Can you give us an overview of your services?		
How long have you been in business?		
What services are available and at what charges?		
Is there a deposit required to reserve your services for our date? What is the percentage?		
When will we need to pay the balance? Do you accept credit cards?		
Could you outline your cancellation policy?		
How many hours will you be at our event?		
If you are ill, who will film our wedding?		
Do you primarily film weddings?		

What other types of videography have you done, or still do?		
What is your style?		
Can we see a video of one entire wedding?		
What other wedding styles of you have done?		
Do you have liability insurance? What does it cover?		
Do you bring back up equipment?		
Can we see a wedding shot similar to our style?		
When do you first start filming?		
Do you ever turn off your camera?		
Do we help edit or do you decide what to cut?		
How soon after the event do we get videos?		

How many meetings could we have with you?		
How many hours of footage will be taken?		
How much footage will we get to see?		
What percentage of the video will be ceremony and reception?		
Do you video mostly us, guests, key events?		
How is "face time" divided per person?		
Can we give you a list of people to film?		
Can we give you a list of people NOT to film?		
Do you capture key events from separate angles; with 2+ cameras?		
If not, is that an option? What would that fee be?		
How many cameras will you bring?		

Do you use a tripod for the ceremony?		
Are you inconspicuous at the wedding?		
Will you film at the rehearsal and dinner? What is that fee?		
Will you come early on the day of to video us getting ready? Is that included in the fee or is that extra?		
Do you ever zoom in?		
How do overtime charges works, if any apply?		
How many videographers and assistants attend the wedding?		
If others will be shooting footage can we see their work?		
Do you and your staff require meals?		
What will your attire be?		
Are there any extra charges? (Travel, etc)		

Do you have a formal education in videography?		
Where did you acquire your education?		
Can you set up a video booth for guests during cocktail hour/reception?		
Will you help create a video to play at the cocktail hour?		
Do you have equipment for that? Screen and projector?		
How soon will you need the footage to put that together for us? If not, can you help us make our own?		
Can we use your equipment if we make our own montage?		
How do you accommodate last minute changes?		
How many weddings do you film a year?		
Can you refer us to any vendors you have worked with in the past?		
What is the biggest problem you've ever had? How was it resolved?		

Can you provide a list of couples you have worked with that we can call?		

Editing, Videos, Packages		
	Option 1	Option 2
Can we create our own package of your services to best fit our needs?		
How many videos are included in the fee?		
Is the final copy uncut or edited?		
What are our length options for videos? How long is each video?		
What is the cost for each additional video?		
Are all the videos the same length?		
Do you offer shorter parent/party videos?		
Do you edit the film or send it to a company?		
How do you transition between scenes?		
Will our video be edited by the same person as the demo we will watch?		
Do we get to keep the raw footage as part of the package?		

If not, can we buy it, or will you always own it?		
If you keep it, for how long do you keep it?		
Do we have choices for video segment styles?		
Can we see different video styles?		
Can you put music over scenes? And titles? What is that fee?		
What sort of special effects can we add? What is that fee?		
Is there an extra fee to put our names and date on the video cover?		
Can we give you baby/honeymoon footage to add in the videos? What is that fee?		
How soon will you need the footage to put that together for us?		

The Flavor

Things to consider before scheduling an interview with your caterer and cake baker:

1. Style! How do you want food to be served or presented?
    - American: Food is plated in the kitchen and brought to guests that are seated at each table
    - Buffet: Food is organized on long tables and guests go through putting food on their own plates
    - Family: Food is placed on large platters and centered on each table so guests serve themselves
    - French: Serving teams who prepares meals tableside and serve food onto plates that are already set

2. Structure! How do you want your cake to look?
    - Tiers: two? Multiple? Columns? Cake stand?
    - Icing or Fondant? How many fillings? What flavors?
    - Decoration: Piping? Real flowers or gum paste?
    - Alternatives: Cupcakes, sheet cake, Groom's Cake?

Questions to ask a Caterer...

Option 1: _____   Option 2: _____
Contact Name: _____   Contact Name: _____
Contact Number: _____   Contact Number: _____
Appointment date/time: _____   Appointment date/time: _____

	Option 1	Option 2
Can you give us an overview of your services?		
How long have you been in business?		
What services are offered and at what charges?		
How many hours will you be at our event?		
How many of those hours are meant for setup/cleanup?		
Are gratuities included in the total quote?		
Is there a deposit required to reserve your services for our date? What is the percentage?		
When will we need to pay the balance? Do you accept credit cards?		
Could you outline your cancellation policy?		

Do you have liability insurance?		
Do you offer all styles of food service? (buffet, sit down, station)		
What service items do you provide (tables, linens, china, glassware)?		
Are there choices for the provided items?		
Is there a rental deposit for breakage & stains? Would we get that back?		
If you do not have service items, do you rent them?		
Will you provide a list of items needed?		
How many guests fit per table (if provided)?		
Can tables and linens easily be setup by you? How are they arranged?		
How are setup & cleanup handled?		
How does flow work if several areas are used?		

If on-site cater: Who will be the chef on duty for our event?		
Are there set menu packages and are they customizable?		
What menu would you suggestion for our budget, for both cocktail hour and dinner?		
Where and when will cocktails be served?		
Will guests be offered two entrée options?		
Do you offer special meal requests (vegetarian)?		
How do you accommodate last minute changes?		
Will you/the chef prepare family recipes?		
Do you offer tasting to help select the menu?		
Is there an additional charge for tastings?		
Will tastings be made by the same person cooking for the wedding?		

Are there a minimum number of plates that must be ordered?		
Do you offer meals for other service providers working at our wedding?		
Do you offer children's meals at a lower price?		
How many meetings can we have with you?		
When do you need to have a final head count?		
Is a traditional wedding cake extra if we order through you? And a groom's cake?		
If we get a cake from a private baker, do you charge a cutting fee?		
Is champagne for a toast included? If not, what is the additional charge?		
How do bar fees work?		
Are fees based on opened bottles or consumption?		
Are there rules regarding alcohol? Are soda/tonics provided at no charge?		

Are refunds given for unopened bottles?		
Could we do a "Signature Drink" at the reception?		
Can we provide our own bar supplies? Is there a corkage fee?		
Who will oversee the wait staff and kitchen on our wedding day?		
How long has the staff worked together?		
How will the staff be dressed?		
What is the server/guest ratio?		
If off-site: Have you worked at our site?		
If so, how does it meet your needs? If not, do you plan to visit it?		
Are there ample electrical outlets to support your needs?		
Has the venue ever blown a fuse? How was it fixed?		

Are other decorations permitted?		
How many weddings do you serve a year?		
Will you ever do more than one wedding on the same day? Same time?		
Is there someone on staff to help cue the day of events (service, etc)?		
Can you refer us to any vendors you have worked with in the past?		
What is the biggest problem you have had? How was it resolved?		
Can you provide a list of couples who have used your services?		

Questions to ask a Cake Baker...

Option 1: _____   Option 2: _____
Contact Name: _____   Contact Name: _____
Contact Number: _____   Contact Number: _____
Appointment date/time: _____   Appointment date/time: _____

	Option 1	Option 2
Please give us an overview of your services?		
What services are available and at what charges for our date?		
What are our size options for cakes?		
Could you make a sheet cake to serve to guests in addition to the wedding cake?		
What are our options for shapes of cake?		
What are our cake, filling, icing, and decoration options?		
Do you have cake stands, pillars, toppers, etc?		
Do you offer tasting to help select the cake? Is there an additional charge for tastings?		
How many cake samples will we get to taste?		

Will tastings be prepared by the same person baking our cake?		
Do you offer a Groom's cake, or cupcakes?		
Is there a discount on those if you do our cake?		
What is the mark up for fondant, and marzipan?		
Will you do piping? At what additional cost?		
Do you work with flowers? Edible or not? If not will you work with our florist?		
How long can the cake be in the sun? Outside?		
How many hours will you be at our event?		
Can we give you pictures or magazine clippings to show you our vision? Or will you make a custom design for us?		
Will you deliver and set up the cake? How much is delivery? When will you arrive?		
How many of those hours are meant for setup/cleanup?		

Is there an extra fee for you to stay and cut and serve the cake?		
If not an option, can you offer instructions to our catering staff?		
Is the top tier included in the serving count?		
What are some of the styles of weddings you have done in the past?		
Is there a deposit required to reserve your services for our date? What is the percentage?		
When will we need to pay the balance? Do you accept credit cards?		
How long have you been in business?		
Could you outline your cancellation policy?		
Do you have liability insurance? What does it cover?		
What service items do you provide (knife & server, stand)?		
Are there choices for the provided items?		

Is there a rental deposit for breakage & stains?		
If you do not have service items, do you rent them?		
Will you provide a list of items needed?		
What are the fees for the cake we're interested in and what do they include?		
Can you refer us to any vendors you have worked with?		
What is the biggest problem you have had? How was it resolved?		
Can you provide a list of couples who have recently used your venue that we can call?		

The Party

Things to consider before scheduling an interview with your DJ and Musicians:

A great event is formed around the entertainment, which will in fact make or break the party.

- It's a good idea to hear the band/DJ that you are considering perform at an event similar to yours. This way you can feel their style and the overall impression they make
- When selecting music, consider a range of songs so that there is something for everyone
- Discuss where in the reception space the band or DJ will be stationed and where the speakers will be; you don't want the speakers too close to the tables, especially those where the elderly guests are sitting

Questions to ask a Disc Jockey...

Option 1: _____   Option 2: _____
Contact Name: _____   Contact Name: _____
Contact Number: _____   Contact Number: _____
Appointment date/time: _____   Appointment date/time: _____

	Option 1	Option 2
Please give us an overview of your services?		
How long have you been in business?		
What options do we have and at what charges?		
How many hours will you be at our event?		
How many of those hours are music and how many are setup/breakdown?		
How early do you arrive on the day of to setup?		
How do overtime charges work? Would any apply?		
Is there a deposit required to reserve your services for our date?		
When will we need to pay the balance? Do you accept credit cards?		

Could you outline your cancellation policy?		
Do you have liability insurance?		
Do you work weddings primarily?		
What is your style?		
What are some wedding styles of you have done in the past?		
How many meetings will we have with you?		
If you're ill, who will DJ our wedding?		
Will you offer a list of songs to choose from?		
Are you willing to play songs that are not in your collection?		
Will you obtain the songs we want or do we give you a CD?		
Do you have the traditional songs?		

Do you have our type of music in your collection?		
Will you take requests from guests?		
Can we give you a list of songs we want played?		
Can we give you a list of songs we DON'T played?		
Will you be the master of ceremonies?		
How do you transition between key events?		
When do you typically first start playing?		
Do you motivate the crowd, or do you limit the talking?		
Can you be inconspicuous during the wedding?		
Also at the reception?		
Do you have any group dances of contests in your repertoire?		

Will you refrain from doing these if we wish?		
How many breaks do you require? At what length?		
Will music play during the breaks?		
Will you play during the cocktail hour?		
Is there an additional fee or discount?		
What other types of events have you done?		
Have you ever been to our wedding venue(s)?		
If so, how does it meet your needs? If not, do you plan to visit it?		
Does our site have the facilities you need?		
Are there ample electrical outlets to support your needs?		
What kind of equipment do you use? Is it top of the line? Do you have backup equipment?		

How many microphones do you have?		
Are your microphones wireless?		
Do you provide microphones for the ceremony?		
Do you have separate sound equipment for the ceremony and reception?		
How do you ensure all of the vows are heard?		
What sort of special effects can we add?		
What would that fee be?		
Do you have equipment to play a video montage if we provide you footage? Screen and projector, or televisions?		
Is there an extra fee?		
How many DJ's and assistants will be there?		
What will you wear?		

Do you and your staff require meals?		
Are there any extra charges? (Travel, etc)		
Can we come see you in action at an event?		
Do you have a formal education in music? Where did you acquire your education?		
How do you deal with last minute changes?		
How many weddings do you DJ a year?		
Can you refer us to any vendors you have worked with?		
What is the biggest problem you've ever had? How was it resolved?		
Can you provide a list of couples who have recently used your venue that we can call?		

Questions to ask Musicians or Bands...

Option 1: _____   Option 2: _____
Contact Name: _____   Contact Name: _____
Contact Number: _____   Contact Number: _____
Appointment date/time: _____   Appointment date/time: _____

	Option 1	Option 2
What services are available and at what charges?		
Is there a deposit required to reserve your services for our date? What is the percentage?		
When will we need to pay the balance?		
Do you accept credit cards?		
Could you outline your cancellation policy?		
What is your style?		
How long have you been playing together?		
Will the musicians we're hearing be those playing at our wedding?		
How long have you played your instrument?		

What are some wedding styles of you have done in the past?		
Can we hear samples of your work?		
Do you have our type of music in your collection?		
Are you willing to play songs that are not in your collection?		
Can we give you a list of songs we want played?		
Can we give you a list of songs we DON'T want to be played?		
Do you have traditional songs that we want?		
Do you provide a list of songs to choose from?		
Will you obtain the songs we want or do we give you sheet music?		
Will you take requests from guests?		
What songs would work best with our wedding?		

Do you primarily work weddings?		
How early do you arrive on the day of to setup?		
When do you typically first start playing?		
How many hours will you be at our event?		
How many of the hours are music and setup/breakdown?		
How many breaks do you require, and at what lengths?		
Will recorded music play during the breaks?		
Will you play during the cocktail hour?		
Do you use microphones? How many microphones do you have?		
Do you have separate sound equipment for the ceremony and reception?		
What kind of equipment do you use? Is it top of the line?		

Do you have backup equipment?		
How do you transition between key events?		
Are there any extra charges? (Travel, etc)		
What other types of events have you done?		
Are you inconspicuous during the wedding?		
Do you require anything from us at the ceremony? Chair to sit in, bottled water, dinner?		
What will you wear?		
Can we come see you in action at an event?		
Do you have liability insurance?		
Do you have a formal education in music?		
Where did you acquire your education?		

How many meetings can have with you?		
Do you and your group require meals?		
If you're ill, who will play at our wedding?		
How do overtime charges work?		
What is the biggest problem you've had? How was it resolved?		
How do you deal with last minute changes?		
Can you provide a list of couples you have worked for in the past to call?		
Can you refer us to any vendors you like working with?		

Love in Bloom

Things to consider before scheduling an interview with your florists:

- Bring pictures of floral arrangements with you to help convey your vision
- Make sure centerpieces do not obstruct your guests' view of one another
- Avoid flowers with powerful scents as they may interfere with guests' enjoyment of the food
- Ask you attendants if they are allergic to any flowers

Things you might need from your florist:

Bride's bouquet, tossing bouquet, Bridesmaids' bouquets, boutonnieres, corsages, centerpieces, altar arrangements, aisle arrangements, hairpieces, flower girl petals, cake flowers, topiaries, arbor garlands, tossing petals, food & guest book table(s) arrangements

Rentals a Florist may have: vases, Sheppard hooks, baskets, lanterns, arbors pillars, columns, wreaths, garlands, tiki torches and more!

Questions to ask a Florist...

Option 1: _____   Option 2: _____
Contact Name: _____   Contact Name: _____
Contact Number: _____   Contact Number: _____
Appointment date/time: _____   Appointment date/time: _____

	Option 1	Option 2
Can you give us an overview of your services?		
What services are available, and at what charges?		
Will you look at pictures we've found to help explain our vision?		
Will you create a design based on our vision?		
How many meetings do we have with you?		
Is there a deposit required to reserve your services for our date? What is the percentage?		
When will we need to pay the balance? Do you accept credit cards?		
Could you outline your cancellation policy?		
How long have you been in business?		

Can we see photos of flowers you have done?		
What other wedding styles of you have done?		
Do you have a portfolio we can select from?		
Do you have a certain style you always use?		
Can we see sample arrangements?		
Where do you get the flowers for your arrangements?		
Are arrangements made the day of, before?		
Do you arrange centerpieces in vases at the site when you arrive or at your shop?		
If we are renting our vases from another source when will you need them?		
Are there delivery and setup fees?		
What time will flowers be delivered and when do you arrive to setup?		

Will you be on hand the day of the wedding to set up or will someone else do that?		
If someone else, can we see his/her work?		
How are arrangements stored?		
What will the different costs be for the elements we are interested in?		
Do in-season flowers affect the costs at all?		
Will the flowers we are interested in be in-season for our wedding?		
If not can you suggest similar looking flowers that are in season to save money?		
Do you offer money saving tips?		
Do you have access to all flower types?		
How far in advance of the Big Day do we need to place our order?		
How long do the arrangements last on the wedding day? After?		

Do you provide preservations for the bridal bouquet?		
Can we make a smaller tossing bouquet?		
Can we order flower petals from you for the aisle? Or cake?		
Are you familiar with safety issues and edible flowers?		
What if you don't have what we want in stock?		
How do you incorporate flowers into a theme?		
What level of blooms will you use to make our arrangements?		
Will all flowers be in full bloom on our day?		
Have you ever done "living centerpieces"?		
How many weddings do you design for a year?		
Do you specialize in weddings?		

Will you ever provide for more than one wedding on the same day?		
How many events are you doing on our date?		
What other types of events have you done?		
How do you feel about transforming ceremony arrangements into centerpieces?		
Could we buy other floral accessories at a wholesale price through you for other projects?		
Can we order/rent decorative shrubbery or trees from you?		
Have you ever done submerged centerpieces?		
Do you design floral hair pieces?		
Do you ever work with herbs or spices as decoration?		
Can you design an Oregon floral theme?		
Have you ever used green or black flowers?		

Do you do floral favors?		
Do you provide candles and displays with them?		
How long will the flowers last out of water?		
Do you have any formal education in flower arranging?		
How do you cope with last minute changes?		
Can you refer us to vendors you have worked with in the past?		
What is the biggest problem you have had? How was it resolved?		
Can you give us a list of couples who recently used your services?		

Boutonnieres	Groomsmen	Ushers/Ring Bearer	Fathers	Family
Needed				
Corsages	Attendants	Honored Guest	Mothers	Family
Needed				
Arrangements	Aisle	Altar	Centerpieces	Tables
Needed				

Vases & Rentals		
	Option 1	Option 2
Do you provide any other rental items? Lanterns, vase fillers, etc:		
If we provide vases, how soon will you need them? Can we have them waiting for you at the site on the Big Day?		
Is there an additional fee to rent the vases?		
Are the vases ours to keep, or do they need to be returned to you?		
When do we return them after the wedding?		
Can we provide our own?		
If we want to give away the centerpieces, can we buy the vases from you?		

Notes

_____

_____

_____

_____

_____

_____

_____

_____

_____

Fashion

Things to consider before scheduling an interview with your Bridal Salon and other Attire providers:

- If making an appointment on the weekend, request an early time and still be prepared to wait
- Try on a variety of dress styles; dresses often look either better on you, or better on the hanger
- The groom might want to consider purchasing a tuxedo rather than renting one; by figuring out how much use he would get out of it and looking into how many times he would need to rent one.
  - The cost of purchasing may be lower than several rentals in the long run!
- If the groom doesn't want to wear a tuxedo, consider a dark suit to wear in coordinating with the formality. For more casual events a dark blazer and neutral trousers will suffice.
- If renting, the groom and groomsmen should pick up their ensembles a few days early in preparation for any mistakes or fitting errors.
- Men should wear either a pocket square or boutonniere, not both.

Bridal Needs: Things to consider buying or renting

Item	Size	Option 1		Option 2	
		Price	Color	Price	Color
Gown					
Veil/Headpiece					
Shoes (have before first fitting)					
Undergarments (have before first fitting)					
Garter & Purse					
Earrings & Necklace					
Hair Accessories					
Going-Away Outfit					
Rehearsal Dinner Outfit					
Totals					

	Option 1	Option 2
Something Borrowed		
Something Blue		
Something Old		
Something New		

Questions to ask before a Bridal Salon Appointment...

Option 1: _____   Option 2: _____
Contact Name: _____   Contact Name: _____
Contact Number: _____   Contact Number: _____
Appointment date/time: _____   Appointment date/time: _____

	Option 1	Option 2
Can you give us an overview of your services?		
Are there any Specials or Sales going on now?		
How long have you been in business?		
What services are included with the cost?		
Do you carry insurance? What does it cover?		
Is there a deposit required to order a gown? What is the percentage?		
Do you sell accessories such as veils, shoes?		
Are there any specials on accessories if I buy my gown from you?		
What is the price range of dresses here?		

Would I have to purchase those accessories on the same day/at the same time I purchase my gown?		
When do I to pay the balance? Do you accept credit cards? What is the cancellation policy?		
How long does it take to order a gown?		
Will we be assigned a sales associate, or will I try on gowns on my own?		
Can I bring pictures of gowns I have seen so that you can tell me if you carry them or for you to see what I like?		
Will you look at pictures I've found to help explain my vision?		
Will I look through your selection of gowns and decide what I want to try on? Or will a sales associate decide what to show me?		
Is there a limit to dresses I can try on?		
Do I need to bring special undergarments and shoes to try on dresses, or do you provide these?		
If you don't have the dress I want, is there a portfolio/catalogue we can select from?		
Do you provide alterations? Are they included in the cost? If not, can you refer us to someone who can?		

Do you provide cleaning and preservations for the dress? Can you refer us to someone who can?		
Do you offer discounts for bridesmaids if I purchase my gown here?		
Does someone dye shoes to match the dress?		
Can I hire someone to bustle the dress?		
Do you deliver?		

Questions to ask about the Gown when in the salon...

	Option 1	Option 2
Which dress and style do you suggest for my body shape?		
Are some styles better for certain seasons?		
Are some fabrics better for certain seasons?		
Can any of the designs I try on be customized?		
Are some dresses available in more than one fabric? Color?		
Are there less expensive fabric alternatives?		
How much is the gown that I am interested in?		
What all does the gown's price include?		
How much are alterations?		
How many fittings will I get to have?		
How far in advance must I place the order?		
Do you steam the dress after final alterations? When will it be ready?		

Questions to ask about Bridesmaid's Dresses...

	Option 1	Option 2
What styles do you suggest for a group of different body shapes?		
How do you handle orders and fittings for bridesmaids who live out-of-town?		
Do you have pictures of dresses to send them?		
How soon do we need to place our order?		
How long after we place our order will the dresses arrive?		
If we are receiving a discount because I bought my dress here, and the bridesmaid wants to order a different dress than the others, will she still receive the discount?		
If you do alterations, are they included in the price of the dress?		
If not, what is the cost?		
Can you refer us to someone who can?		
How much is the dress?		
How much is the deposit? When will we need to pay the balance?		

Questions to ask about the Men's Attire...

Option 1: _____   Option 2: _____
Contact Name: _____   Contact Name: _____
Contact Number: _____   Contact Number: _____
Appointment date/time: _____   Appointment date/time: _____

	Option 1	Option 2
Do we need to make an appointment or can we just walk in?		
How far in advance do we need to reserve the groom's suit and the groomsmen's suits?		
What different styles and colors do you offer?		
How old is the attire that you rent out?		
Will my ushers receive a discount on their suits if I order mine from here?		
What is the cost of each suit or ensemble?		
What is included as part of the entire ensemble?		
How do fittings work?		
Can groomsmen just drop in at their convenience to be fitted in the suits we have selected for them?		

Will groomsmen pay for their suits when they pick them up or at their final fittings?		
Are the suits pressed?		
Do you sell/rent shoes and accessories?		
What is the payment policy? Do you accept credit cards?		
What is the cancellation policy? When will we need to pay the balance?		
Will we incur extra charges if the suits are damaged, or do you assume there will be some ware and tear?		
When can we pick it up?		
When will the suits need to be returned?		

Getting Pretty

Things to consider before scheduling an interview with your Hair and Makeup artists:

- Even if you don't usually wear much makeup, it is wise to have your makeup done professionally for your Big Day. You will feel beautiful and special, and a professional will know how to make you look stunning in your photographs
- Be sure to purchase the same shade of lipstick that the artist will put on you for touch ups on the Big Day
- Wear a button-down shirt when you get your hair and makeup done to avoid smudges and tangles when changing.
- Avoid having any treatments for the 2 weeks prior to the Big Day.
- Do treat yourself to a manicure and pedicure. You'll want your hands to look as lovely as that ring you'll be showing off! The pedicure will be great for your honeymoon too.

Questions to ask a Hair Stylist & Makeup Artist...

Option 1: _____   Option 2: _____
Contact Name: _____   Contact Name: _____
Contact Number: _____   Contact Number: _____
Appointment date/time: _____   Appointment date/time: _____

If obtaining both services from the same salon:

	Option 1	Option 2
How long have you been in business?		
What are some of the services available and at what charges?		
When can we schedule a trial run? What if I don't like the trial run? Will we keep scheduling until I find a hair style I do like?		
Will you travel? Is there an additional charge for you to come to us at the venue?		
Is there a deposit required to reserve your services for our date? What is the percentage?		
When will we need to pay the balance? Do you accept credit cards?		
What should I wear to get my hair and makeup done?		
Do you prefer clean hair yesterday's hair?		
Do you wash and rise hair on the Big Day or should I shower in the morning?		

Should my hair be dry or damp when I arrive?		
Will you try styling my hair to match any magazine clipping styles I bring in?		
What sort of hairstyle do you recommend for my face shape, hair length and gown neck line?		
Do you have a certain length of hair you work best with?		
Is my hair thick enough to achieve the look I want, or can you put in temporary extensions?		
How much do extensions cost and when would I need to get them put in?		
Do I need to cut my hair or grow it out for a while to achieve the certain hair style I am looking for?		
Do you carry insurance? What does it cover?		
Will you stay on hand to help with my hair and veil after the ceremony?		
Will you teach me how to remove my veil?		
Who will work with us if you are ill on our date?		

What kind of space and lighting do you need?		
Do you bring your own equipment and products?		
Will you bring an assistant? Can I meet with your assistant? Do they do styling on their own, or just help?		
Will you style mine and my attendants' hair or will your assistant?		
How long will it take to have our hair/face done?		
Do you mind if the photographer or videographer is present at our appointment?		
If you won't be at the site, can you provide me with products to do my own touchups?		

If Makeup Artist is separate...

Option 1: _____   Option 2: _____
Contact Name: _____   Contact Name: _____
Contact Number: _____   Contact Number: _____
Appointment date/time: _____   Appointment date/time: _____

	Option 1	Option 2
What services available and at what charges?		
How long have you been in business?		
When can we schedule a trial run? What if I don't like the trial run? Will we keep scheduling until I find makeup I do like?		
Will you travel? Is there an additional charge for you to come to us at the venue?		
Is there a deposit required to reserve your services for our date? What is the percentage?		
When will we need to pay the balance? Do you accept credit cards?		
What is the cancellation policy?		
Do you carry insurance? What does it cover?		
Will you stay to help with touchups after the ceremony?		

Would there be an additional fee for that?		
If you won't be at the site, can you provide me with products to do my own touchups?		
Do you bring your own makeup or use mine?		
What kind of space and lighting do you need?		
Will you bring an assistant?		
Can I meet with your assistant? Do they do makeup on their own, or just help you?		
Who will do our makeup if you are ill on our date?		
Who will do my attendants' makeup? You or your assistant?		
How long will it take to have my makeup done?		
How long will it take to have the attendants' makeup done?		
Can hair and makeup done at the same time?		

Do you mind if the photographer or videographer is present at our appointment?		
What should we wear when we have our appointment?		
What color eye makeup do you suggest for my skin tone and hair color?		

Practice Makes Perfect

Things to consider before scheduling an interview with your rehearsal dinner site and caterer:

- When hosting a Rehearsal Dinner, the immediate family should be evenly dispersed amongst the tables to better host guests.
- Be sure that the area is accessible and safe for all guests (wheelchairs, crutches, small children)
- If your Officiant is not paid, you should invite him/her and spouse to the rehearsal dinner, especially if they are attending the rehearsal

Questions to ask a Rehearsal Dinner Venue...

Option 1: _____   Option 2: _____
Contact Name: _____   Contact Name: _____
Contact Number: _____   Contact Number: _____
Appointment date/time: _____   Appointment date/time: _____

	Option 1	Option 2
What dates and times are you available?		
Is there a deposit required to reserve your services for our date? What is the percentage?		
What is your cancellation policy? When will we need to pay the balance?		
What is the overall fee and what exactly does that include?		
By reserving the site for a private party, do we get a discount on the menu?		
Do you have a specific menu you always use for large parties and dinners?		
Can you work with our menu to keep it different than that which will be served at our wedding?		
Can you cater to special dietary needs?		
Do you offer a buffet or a seated meal?		

How many people does the space hold? Seated and Standing?		
How many hours are we allotted? Do overtime charges apply?		
Is an open bar included in the site fee or menu estimate?		
Is there a bar where guests can order and pay for their own drinks?		
Can we bring in our own beverages?		
Are wait staff and bar tender gratuities included in the site fee?		
Will there be a maitre d' assigned to our party?		
Will there be a wait staff assigned to our party?		
When will you need a final head count? Is there a minimum head count required?		
How many guests can sit at each table?		
What is the server to guest ratio?		

How private is the space we'll be using?		
Are there outdoor spaces we can use?		
If an outdoor location: Is there a plan for inclement weather? An indoor alternative?		
Is there someone on staff to help plan and coordinate the rehearsal dinner?		
How many rehearsal dinners do you host a year?		
Will you ever do more than one dinner on the same day? Same time?		
When can we get into the site to decorate?		
When must we take down any decorations?		
Do you provide any sort of table decorations?		
Can we hang decorations from the ceiling?		
What does the lighting look like at night?		

Can we bring in decorations? Are other decorations permitted?		
Is there an open flame restriction on candles?		
Can we visit the space when it is setup?		
Is there a space for musicians to set up? How are the acoustics?		
Are there ample electrical outlets to support their needs?		
Is there a coat check; at what extra cost if any?		
Is there valet parking; at what extra cost if any?		
Does the facility have liability insurance? What does it cover?		
Will our area be wheelchair accessible?		
Can you refer us to any vendors you have worked with in the past?		
What is the biggest problem you have had? How was it resolved?		

Going Somewhere?

Things to consider before scheduling interviews with hotels and your transportation services:

Your Wedding Night:

- Do you want a grand suite with a Jacuzzi and room service or a modest Bed N' Breakfast in the country?
- How will you get to your warm bed after the reception?
- Who will decorate and will you want it decorated?

Transportation:

- Before booking the car service inspect the cars, preferably the actual one that you will be using. Examine seats, seat belts, paint condition, etc. Then write down the license plate numbers of the specific cars you rent for your day. Put them in the contract!
- A stretch limo is a great option with a lot of room, but don't forget about a unique way such as a vintage car, or horse drawn carriage. If you do go a unique route, make sure the photographer is informed and doesn't miss your entry or exit.
- If there are any restrictions on decorating your car, be sure to inform your attendants beforehand.
- Be sure to enlist the services of a shuttle company for after the reception to reduce the risks of drinking and driving.

Questions to ask about Wedding Night Reservation...

Option 1: _____   Option 2: _____
Contact Name: _____   Contact Name: _____
Contact Number: _____   Contact Number: _____
Appointment date/time: _____   Appointment date/time: _____

	Option 1	Option 2
Is there a Honeymoon Suite? Is it available on our wedding night?		
Can we see the suite?		
What is the rate of this suite? What are the rates for other rooms on our wedding night?		
Can we see the other rooms?		
Is there a deposit required to reserve the room for our date? What is the percentage?		
When will we need to pay the balance? What is your cancellation policy?		
If our guests are staying at this hotel do we get any special rates?		
When is check-out? Can we get a later time?		
Can you give us an overview of any unique perks or services?		

Are there any special amenities in the suite?		
Is breakfast included?		
Is there room service?		
Are the rooms air-conditioned/heated?		
Can we send someone to decorate the suite?		
When can we get into the suite to decorate?		

Questions to ask about Guest Accommodations...

Option 1: _____   Option 2: _____
Contact Name: _____   Contact Name: _____
Contact Number: _____   Contact Number: _____
Appointment date/time: _____   Appointment date/time: _____

	Option 1	Option 2
Do you offer special rates for guests?		
What is the regular rate and what is the discounted rate?		
How many rooms can we hold in one block?		
How many rooms at the special rate are available on the dates we need?		
Can we see the rooms?		
Do we incur any charges if not all of the rooms in the block are actually booked by guests?		
Are there a minimum number of rooms that must be booked by guests for all to receive the special rate?		
Is there a minimum nights they must stay?		
Is there a date by which guests must reserve the rooms to receive the special rate?		

Do you offer a shuttle service between the hotel and airport?		
What amenities are available to guests?		
Are the rooms air-conditioned/heated?		
Is breakfast included?		
What amenities and bed sizes are in each room?		
Is there room service?		
What is the check-out time? Can it be extended?		
What are the views from the rooms in the discounted block?		
Will guests have the choice of single or double beds per room in the block?		
Can we get into the rooms prior to guests' arrivals and leave Welcome Baskets, or can you do that for us?		
Could we have guests receive the Welcome Baskets from the front desk at check in?		

Is there a deposit required to reserve the block of rooms for our date? What is the percentage?		
If the rooms are not reserved by our guests, are we required to pay for them for each night?		
When will we need to pay the balance? What is your cancellation policy?		

Notes

_____

_____

_____

_____

Questions to ask about Transportation Services...

Option 1: _____   Option 2: _____

Contact Name: _____   Contact Name: _____

Contact Number: _____   Contact Number: _____

Appointment date/time: _____   Appointment date/time: _____

	Option 1	Option 2
What is the shuttle fee for guests between two locations?		
What is the shuttle fee for the bridal party between the ceremony and reception venues?		
What is the fee for a "Get-away" ride?		
Are the gratuities already included?		
Can you give us an overview of any unique perks or services?		
What types of cars/vehicles are available on our date?		
Are there vintage cars that we could use for our "get-away" vehicle		
Would we have to hire a driver, or could we have a family member drive?		
Do you offer buses, vans, or shuttle vehicles that run between a parking lot and our venue location?		

How many passengers can the each vehicle comfortably seat?		
Is there a minimum number of hours required?		
What amenities does the fee include?		
How many hours does the rate include?		
If hourly: When does the clock start? - When the driver leaves the lot or when they pick up passengers?		
What are the charges for any amenities that aren't included (champagne, etc)		
How old are the vehicles? Can we see the vehicles?		
How long has each driver been with you?		
How about the ones who will work our events?		
Are your drivers familiar with the area?		
Do you and all of your drivers have insurance?		
What sort of deposit is required to reserve transportation for our wedding date?		

When will we need to pay the balance?		
Please outline your cancellation policy?		
How do you cope with last minute changes?		
Can you refer us to other vendors you have worked with?		
What is the biggest problem you have had?		
How was it resolved?		
Can you give us a list of couples who recently used your services?		

Questions to ask your Travel Agent...

Option 1: _____   Option 2: _____
Contact Name: _____   Contact Name: _____
Contact Number: _____   Contact Number: _____
Appointment date/time: _____   Appointment date/time: _____

	Option 1	Option 2
How long has this agency been in business?		
Do you specialize in any specific type of vacation?		
What do your services include?		
Can you give us an overview of any unique perks or services you offer?		
Do you have relationships with destinations that give your clients discounts?		
Do we book everything through you or do you just tell us where to look and who to talk to?		
Is there a deposit required to reserve our reservations? When will we need to pay the balance?		
What is your cancellation policy?		
Have you visited the destination we're considering?		

Have you sent many couples to any one particular resort?		
Are there any benefits to booking our reservations this far in advance?		
Are there are down falls we should consider when booking our reservations this far in advance?		
Do you have any photos/brochures of potential hotels? Including a picture of the room?		
What is the cost of the trip we're interested in and what is included?		
Will we need to get any vaccines before we go?		
What is the currency where we are in going?		
Do you offer exchange rate accommodations?		
What type of travel insurance is offered? What is the extra cost?		
Can you schedule activities and reservations for the days we are on our honeymoon?		

Appendix A: Rental Items Needed

Rental Item	Vendor 1				Vendor 2			
	Description	Cost/ Item	Qty.	Total Cost	Description	Cost/ Item	Qty.	Total Cost
CEREMONY								
Chairs								
Chair Covers								
Chair Sashes								
Chuppah/Canopy								
Columns or pillars								
Altar Decor								
Pew bows								
Candelabras								
Unity Candle Holders								
Flower Girl Basket(s)								
Aisle Runner								
Kneeling Bench								
Welcome/Gift Table								
Other								
COCKTAIL HOUR								
Chairs								
Cocktail Tables								
Guest Tables								
Linens								
China								
Flatware								
Serving Pieces								
Decorative Accessories								
Other								
RECEPTION								
Beverage dispensers								
Bubble Machine								
Canopies								
Centerpieces								
Chafing Dishes								
Chairs								

Chargers								
China								
Cotton Candy Machine								
Dance Floor								
Dance Floor trim								
Decorative Accessories								
Flatware								
Fog machine								
Garbage Cans								
Generator								
Guest Tables								
Head Table								
Heaters								
Karaoke Machine								
Lanterns								
Lights								
Linen Napkins								
Linens								
Photo booth								
Popcorn Machine								
Portable Toilets								
Recycling Stations								
Serving Pieces								
Soda Fountain								
Sweetheart table								
Table Runners								
Tent								
Vases								
Other								
TOTAL								

Best of luck to you in your interviews!
I know many awesome Wedding Professionals and I would love to see you working with them!

All Wedding Professional Communities are tight knit groups and often refer, network and recommend each other. I highly encourage you to choose a Dream Team of vendors who have all worked together often and can be a single presence of Professional Awesomeness on your Big Day.

As a long time coordinator I can tell you that there is nothing quite like observing a wedding {behind the scenes of course} of a Vendor Team who has worked together over and over. The systems, efficiencies and teamwork they develop is certainly worth paying for and selecting them over others. One vendor may be just over your budget, but he/she might be the necessary piece that assembles your perfect Dream Team.
Take it into consideration. You'll be glad you did.

Green-Eyed Girl Productions has several Dream Team Vendors that we recommend. Find them all at www.green-eyedgirlproductions.com